SAM & KEVIN SORBO

SHARE THE LIGHT

40 WORLD-CHANGING DEVOTIONS

BroadStreet
PUBLISHING

BroadStreet Publishing® Group, LLC
Savage, Minnesota, USA
BroadStreetPublishing.com

SHARE THE LIGHT: 40 WORLD-CHANGING DEVOTIONS

Copyright © 2018 Sam and Kevin Sorbo

978-1-4245-5828-5 (Cinedigm softcover)
978-1-4245-5727-1 (e-book)

All rights reserved. No part of this book may be reproduced in any form, except for brief quotations in printed reviews, without permission in writing from the publisher.

Some devotional content is from *Make a Difference* by Ken Castor. Used by permission.

Unless otherwise noted, Scripture quotations are from the Holy Bible, New Living Translation, copyright © 1996, 2004, 2007 by Tyndale House Foundation. Used by permission of Tyndale House Publishers, Inc., Carol Stream, Illinois 60188, USA. All rights reserved. Scripture quotations marked TPT are from The Passion Translation®. Copyright © 2014, 2015, 2016 by BroadStreet Publishing Group, Racine, Wisconsin. thePassionTranslation.com. Used by permission. Scripture quotations marked NKJV are taken from the New King James Version. Copyright © 1982 by Thomas Nelson, Inc. Used by permission. All rights reserved. Scripture quotations marked NIV are taken from the Holy Bible, New International Version®, NIV® Copyright ©1973, 1978, 1984, 2011 by Biblica, Inc.® Used by permission. All rights reserved worldwide.

Stock or custom editions of BroadStreet Publishing titles may be purchased in bulk for educational, business, ministry, fundraising, or sales promotional use. For information, please email info@broadstreetpublishing.com.

Cover design by Chris Garborg at garborgdesign.com
Interior by Katherine Lloyd at theDESKonline.com

Printed in the United States of America

18 19 20 21 22 5 4 3 2 1

Sam and Kevin Sorbo are to be highly recommended for shining the light of their Christian faith in the entertainment industry. Their devotional *Share the Light* can help you be a faithful warrior for the Kingdom so you can change the world!

—*Dr. Ted Baehr, www.movieguide.org*

Kevin and Sam have written encouragement and inspiration into the pages of this book. After the fantastic success of *Let There Be Light*, I can't imagine a better resource than *Share the Light* for making the world a better place!

—*Mike Huckabee, former governor of Arkansas,*
US presidential candidate, best-selling author

Put your feet to your faith! In *Share the Light*, Sam and Kevin creatively inspire readers to effectively improve the world around them. Read it and be empowered!

—*Dr. Robert Jeffress, pastor, First Baptist Church, Dallas*

I found *Share the Light* to be a tremendous resource. It provides powerful words to help us go out and do what our Savior commanded us to do in Mark 16:15—to go out and share the good word with all of creation. I encourage every believer to use this powerful tool in their everyday walk.

—*Michael Franzese, national speaker, author of*
Blood Covenant: The Michael Franzese Story

I really love *Share the Light*! What stuck out to me the most was the consistent message of not keeping the Light to yourself. This devotional is unique in that it encourages us to share God's light with others. Light is impossible to contain. If we have the Light within us, we will not be able to keep it to ourselves. This devotional gives us practical ways to share that Light on a daily basis.

—*Missy Robertson,* Duck Dynasty

Contents

Foreword by Franklin Graham........................ vii
Introduction: The Power of Storytelling............. 1

1	Light in the Darkness......................... 4
2	Feeling Alive................................. 8
3	Help Those in Need........................... 12
4	Put Your Priorities in Place.................. 16
5	Your Presence Has Impact...................... 20
6	Share Your Life with Others................... 24
7	Good News for a Change........................ 28
8	My Light and My Salvation..................... 32
9	What the Lord Does, so Do We.................. 36
10	God Produces Faith in Us..................... 40
11	Another Place................................ 44
12	The Message of Creation...................... 48
13	Sharing God's Love in Times of Grief.......... 52
14	Tempering Your Temper........................ 56
15	Spotlight.................................... 60
16	Cleaning Up Messes........................... 64
17	Your Calling from God........................ 68
18	Life Is Precious............................. 72
19	Make It Real................................. 76
20	Light Shining in Us.......................... 80

21	SHARE YOUR FAITH WITH OTHERS	84
22	LET THERE BE LIGHT	88
23	LIGHT FOR MY PATH	92
24	GOD IS OUR HERO	96
25	THE INTENSITY OF THE LIGHT OF GOD	100
26	THE POWER OF FORGIVENESS	104
27	GOD IS WITH YOU	108
28	UNEXPECTEDLY EXTRAORDINARY	112
29	COMMUNICATING THE LIGHT	116
30	REPRESENTING GOD	120
31	COMMIT YOUR LIFE TO GOD	124
32	WALK IN HIS LIGHT	128
33	THINK OF OTHERS	132
34	OVERCOMING DEATH	136
35	GOD'S PLANS INCLUDE YOU	140
36	SHARE THE GOOD NEWS	144
37	WHOEVER HAS JESUS	148
38	HYPOCRITE-PROOF YOURSELF	152
39	LET YOUR LIGHT SHINE BEFORE OTHERS	156
40	SPREADING THE BAND OF LIGHT	160

AFTERWORD: RESCUE BOATS 164
ACKNOWLEDGMENTS 166
ABOUT THE AUTHORS 166

Foreword

Jesus is the *light* of the world, and He has given us His truth by which we are to live and shine His light in the darkness that falls upon sinful man. For those who believe in and follow the Lord Jesus Christ, we are called to serve Him by living a life that will point others to His forgiveness and His everlasting salvation, for He came to rescue us from the clutches of sin that so easily besets us (Hebrews 12:1).

Who does your heart belong to?

Who do you follow?

Who do you turn to when darkness overshadows and discouragement follows?

Jesus said, "He who follows Me will have the light of life. … As long as I am in the world I am the light of the world" (John 8:12; 9:5).

When Jesus departed from this earth to return to His Father in heaven, He gave us the great privilege and enormous responsibility to be His light. That is not always easy to do because we still struggle with human frailty. At times we may bend to peer pressure and overlook what we know to be wrong. But the Bible tells us that we must become "children of God without fault in the midst of a crooked and perverse generation, among whom you shine as lights in the world" (Philippians 2:15).

You may ask, *How can we do this?* The Bible tells us that the Holy Spirit lives within each believer and will guide and direct our paths if we obey God's Word. Our good works mean nothing if they are not empowered by the Lord Jesus Christ and His truth. When we faithfully speak His Word and follow His commands, it pleases Him to open up ways for our lives to bless others as we speak His name, which brings hope and glorifies the Master of our lives. "For you were once darkness, but now you are light in the Lord. Walk as children of light (for the fruit of the Spirit is in all goodness, righteousness, and truth), finding out what is acceptable to the Lord" (Ephesians 5:8–10).

May God bless you as you seek to honor His mighty name and *Share the Light.*

Franklin Graham
President and CEO
Billy Graham Evangelistic Association
Samaritan's Purse

INTRODUCTION

THE POWER OF STORYTELLING

*What does it profit, my brethren, if someone says
he has faith but does not have works? Can faith save him?
If a brother or sister is naked and destitute of daily food, and
one of you says to them, "Depart in peace,
be warmed and filled," but you do not give them the things
which are needed for the body, what does it profit?
Thus also faith by itself, if it does not have works, is dead.*
James 2:14–17, NKJV

We all love a good story. If it's told well and strikes our emotions, it moves us, stays with us, and affects us in our daily lives. Stories can change the world.

It's very clear that in the Bible, one of the most useful tools that Jesus employs to convey his teachings is the parable—a story that uses consonances and analogies to express some broader or more profound meaning. Jesus effectively changed the world with storytelling, and, as Christian filmmakers, to do that is what Kevin and I also intend. Good stories can move us and affect our thoughts; thoughts compel action, and actions change the world.

After the immense success of the theatrical release of our movie *Let There Be Light*, we decided to produce a book that combines storytelling, devotion to God, reflection on our shared Christian faith, and then action in the public and private domains to change the world for the better.

For instance, the Parable of the Sower paints the picture of seeds

Introduction – The Power of Storytelling

planted in different types of soil. A seed's potential is not fulfilled in the planting but in its growth into a plant. *Let There Be Light* was, for us, like planting seeds. Now we would like to water those seeds with the ideas in this book, to encourage you to flourish both in your faith and in your actions. We would like to watch a veritable forest of light and charitable acts mature out of the initial planting that the movie realized.

James speaks concisely that faith must be accompanied by action. Without action, how will anything change or improve? On a national scale, action changed colonial America into the United States of America. Men, almost all of whom were Christian, with the rest heavily influenced by Christianity, purposed to create a new nation "conceived in liberty and dedicated to the proposition that all men are created equal," as Abraham Lincoln noted in his Gettysburg Address. This accomplishment consequently upended the status quo of one ruler over the many that the world had traditionally embraced for millennia. The variations of emperor, king, dictator, and despot were replaced with a new concept of self-rule, in both the vernacular and in practice. And, subsequently, a surprisingly peaceful transfer of power between two rival political parties occurred, and astonished other governments around the globe, all because of the teachings in our Christian Bible. Loving God and your fellow man was put into action, and it rocked the world.

One notable caveat is John Adams' quote that "Our Constitution was made only for a moral and religious people. It is wholly inadequate to the government of any other." Consider that laws are only as strong as the will of the people to obey them, and once enough members of our society decide to pursue the rule of selfishness (i.e., "What's in it for me?") as opposed to the Golden Rule (i.e., "Do unto others as you would have done unto you."), we will have self-serving rulers at the top creating chaos and tyranny for everyone else. These rulers will demand more powerful, more intrusive, and more controlling policies

INTRODUCTION – THE POWER OF STORYTELLING

and policing to get their self-interests served. We believe that to retain the freedoms we enjoy in this country, we must exercise our Christian faith, both as a way of exhibiting its value to others and because we are called to love our brethren. A great way to do that is by serving others.

You can employ this concept on a daily basis in your own life, and experience its effects and rewards personally. You can create life-changing results, because influencing a single human being always impacts more than just that one.

These are merely suggestions. You can also invent more and even better ways to serve your fellow man and your culture (and posterity). For this reason, there are several prompts in the book to share your stories on social media with the hashtag "LTBL" (#LTBL) to make it easier for people to find them.

The most amazing thing is that when you serve others, give of your time and your resources, and invest emotionally in the welfare of those around you, it leaves you profoundly affected—improved even. While this book is focused on changing the world, it is an unavoidable and extraordinary benefit that when we look outside ourselves to see the bigger picture, the larger story, and the greater suffering that exists beyond our general focus, we begin to re-imagine our role in society and our place in God's creation. We gain perspective that often makes our own troubles pale in comparison. To put it bluntly, serving others is the greatest thing we can do for ourselves, personally.

Through this book, Kevin and I would like to sound that clarion call to action and provide the impetus and the concepts for what those actions might be.

We can change the world, for one person or for many, and through it we transform ourselves as well!

Sam and Kevin Sorbo
January 23, 2018

1

Light in the Darkness

> When Jesus spoke again to the people, he said,
> "I am the light of the world. Whoever follows me will
> never walk in darkness, but will have the light of life."
>
> *John 8:12, NIV*

You are invited on an incredible journey. Ahead of you is a world covered in darkness. Some of your friends and family are stumbling as they stretch out their arms, test their footing, and try to navigate their way through obstacles in the dark. In some moments, debris has covered their paths. In other moments, disoriented wandering has caused them great confusion. People in this darkening world are struggling to see what God has created for them, some, even, fail to know their creator. When darkness sets into a person's life, it steers them a long way from hope and blinds their vision.

But God said, "Let there be light."

And there was.

Jesus, the light of the world, invites you to walk with him as he shines into the darkness. God wants to light the way so that people can find him. He wants you to follow him so that you can have his light of life. As you walk in his steps, he wants you to share his light with others. You are his welcomed partner in his good work to give life to the those faltering in the darkness. His desire is for you to reflect his radiance upon your family, your friends, and all those you will encounter today.

1 – Light in the Darkness

SHINE THE LIGHT

1. Read each word of John 8:12 again. What stands out to you?

2. Take a moment to remember a time you physically walked around in darkness. What did you do with your hands? What was each step like? What worries did you have?

3. What steps could you personally take today to more closely "follow Jesus"?

4. Take a moment to think of friends and family who are struggling today. In what ways are they struggling to find their way in the darkness? How could God's light give them hope?

Lord Jesus, light of the world, thank you for giving light to my life. Thank you for inviting me to join you in your mission. Today, let me reveal your life and light to others. Let me not be afraid. Let me stand tall in the confidence of your good work so that those around me would be given hope. Amen.

Share the Light

Choose someone you know who is clouded by darkness today. Take time right now to pray for them. Brighten up their day by sending them a card, some flowers, or inviting them to do something fun and "light"-hearted with you.

1 – Light in the Darkness

2

Feeling Alive

*For we are God's masterpiece.
He has created us anew in Christ Jesus, so we can
do the good things he planned for us long ago.*

Ephesians 2:10

Too many people in our world don't know how valuable they are. They don't know that there is a God who loves them and is rallying them to stand confidently in his light. Too many people have instead listened to the false narrative of their insignificance. They have been beaten down, and too many people have even convinced themselves that they are not good enough, not special enough, not worthy enough for an abundant life.

As a result, many people deaden their feelings. Hopelessness has a strong and painful grip. But running from problems, as Sol attempted to in the movie *Let There Be Light*, never solves anything. Sol struggled to believe that a God of love would allow any evil in the world. He was wrong, but he enveloped himself in the darkness he felt.

Sol needed a message that there was still hope. He needed to know that God hadn't abandoned him even as he threatened to abandon God. He needed to know that God had purpose for his life. He needed to know he was loved.

SHINE THE LIGHT

1. When someone feels neglected, what impact does that have on their approach to life?

2. When someone feels cherished, what impact does that have on their approach to life?

3. Psalm 139 (NIV) describes humans as being "knit together in the womb" and being "fearfully and wonderfully made." "Your works are wonderful," the psalmist David writes. Take a moment to describe how you have been knit together with God's care and fearfully and wonderfully made with his artistic vision.

4. Do you see others as being made in the image of God? Do you see them as masterpieces? Works of art? How does seeing someone through this lens change the way we would treat others?

Lord, don't let me lose sight of the unique attention you have given my life. In the same way, don't let me lose sight of the intricate detail you have woven in the lives of my neighbors. Let me see people through your precious, artistic lens. Amen.

Share the Light

Gather some friends and, together, try painting or drawing or creating a work of art. As you do, notice how much care and attention goes into the forethought, the materials, the design. Notice how the art reflects you, the creator. Think about to whom you would like this art to go and what message you would like it to convey. With these thoughts in mind, let your friends know how they are God's masterpiece work of art. Share your artwork on social media using #LTBL.

2 – FEELING ALIVE

3

Help Those in Need

Feed the hungry,
and help those in trouble.
Then your light will shine out from the darkness,
and the darkness around you will be as bright as noon.

Isaiah 58:10

I used to volunteer in a very busy emergency room. On every shift, I had to drop my ego on the doorstep as I entered the hospital. Caring for others puts your own problems into perspective. Most of the people were experiencing terrible health crises. They demanded careful attention and compassion, and I could offer them no less than my undivided attention. For my four-hour shift, I was working to help others, and by the time I finished, my own life's problems seemed terribly insignificant. When we are able to help others, that service pulls us out of our own issues and blesses others who need assistance.

Jesus cares deeply for those who are in need. That means our hearts are supposed to embrace their burdens as well. Where Jesus sees darkness, he actively pierces it with his brilliance. He listens for the cry of the hungry and leans into the difficulties of those who are in trouble. He searches for the wounded and lends his shoulders to those in need. He patiently heals and persistently rejoices when people find life through his hands.

When we voluntarily serve others in their times of need, like Jesus, we shine the light of God in the darkness.

3 – Help Those in Need

SHINE THE LIGHT

1. Think back to a time in your life when you were struggling through a difficult situation. For a moment, let yourself remember how it felt to be overwhelmed in that circumstance.

2. Now think back to a specific time when someone came to your aid. How was their support like a light shining in the darkness?

3. Jesus said that he came to serve, not to be served. How would the world be different if more people took this approach to their daily activities?

4. How does serving others impact our own attitude about life?

Lord Jesus, thank you for serving me in my own needs. In times of trouble, you have been ever present with me. I look back at my darkest moments and see that you were there. So now I ask that you use me to bless others who find themselves in difficult circumstances. Let my heart by attentive to those in need and let my hands be ready to serve generously. Amen.

Share the Light

Bring a homeless person a meal, or volunteer to serve at a soup kitchen, and bring a friend with you. Take specific steps today to serve others and share your activities on social media using #LTBL.

3 – HELP THOSE IN NEED

4

PUT YOUR PRIORITIES IN PLACE

Now all glory to God our Father forever and ever! Amen.
Philippians 4:20

Many of us struggle with a need for approval. In our insecurity, we often seek unhealthy affirmation or adoration from those around us. We are tempted to demand respect from our friends, love from our family, recognition from coworkers, and good standing within our community. We strive for conditional, social rewards. Something missing within us longs for acceptance, and so we shift our attention to the accolades that this world so teasingly offers.

Sol's story it much the same, seeking solace from his fans, but never finding the satisfaction he needs because his heart yearns for something less superficial, more profound and meaningful—we all do.

Perhaps much of our struggle is that we prefer to place the spotlight on our exterior achievements rather than dealing with our innermost misgivings. It's easy for our priorities to become misguided. If only we would seek our self-confidence from God our Father.

It has been said that the chief end of mankind is to bring glory to God. The honest question that every one of us needs to face is this one: In all sincerity, given the choice, who would I want to see glorified in my life today? Myself? Or God?

4 – Put Your Priorities in Place

Shine the Light

1. Katy faces her terminal illness with three things on her mind, preparing for eternity, fulfilling the "let there be light" directive, and loving her family. If you knew you had only a few months to live what would your priorities be? How would they be different than the priorities you currently keep?

2. If God is to receive all glory, can we still celebrate our achievements? How so?

3. Trick question: What do you need to do to receive God's approval?

4. What activities or thoughts do you have that get in the way of the glory of God being seen in your life?

God, whenever I am swayed to seek my own stance upon your pedestal, remind me of who you are and what my priorities should be. Amen

Share the Light

On one side of a piece of paper, make a list of your priorities. On the other side, make a "To Do" list of your schedule and activities. Do these two lists match-up? Are there items that contradict one another? How could you make these two lists more congruent?

4 – PUT YOUR PRIORITIES IN PLACE

5

Your Presence Has Impact

> So let's not get tired of doing what is good. At just the right time we will reap a harvest of blessing if we don't give up.
>
> *Galatians 6:9*

Do you ever feel discouraged by another person? Do you have someone in your life who pushes the boundaries, speaks disrespectfully, or sabotages your plans? This is certainly how Katy felt in her relationship with Sol. In fact, one of the most common themes of darkness in our world is a sense of discouragement as we interact with someone close to us. Weariness can so easily creep into the daily grind of our endeavors with them.

Even if there are frustrating stretches, though, even if that antagonistic person refuses to cooperate, and even if your plans for them fall flat or your dreams for them escape your control, your presence day after day, week after week, or even year after year, will have a positive effect.

God's work in a person's life is often long-term. Your presence is a reinforcing reminder of that life-changing truth.

More than just about any profound thing you could say, or any great question you could ask, others need you to *be there*. They may not realize it today, but in time they might discover how much they needed you. With stress and upheaval in a person's life, your consistency speaks more loudly than you probably realize in the midst of disappointing times.

5 – YOUR PRESENCE HAS IMPACT

SHINE THE LIGHT

1. Katy's consistent presence in Sol's life became one of the primary reasons Sol was able to turn his life around. Describe the feelings and experiences Katy had to endure during this journey with Sol.

2. Consider how God has not given up on you. In what ways has he always been present in your life, even during those times when you didn't notice?

3. Do you have someone in your life who wears you down? What causes you to grow weary of them? What do you feel you need to help you not give up?

4. Over the long term, what is your prayer for that person? Pause right now to pray.

※

Dear Jesus, I need your strength. I cannot carry the burden of others on my own. Give me wisdom to pace myself and grace to be patient. Give me stamina to continue doing good for those you put on my heart. Amen.

Share the Light

In a nice basket, bring some healthy snacks to your local firehouse or police station, with a note that says "Share the Light" or a Bible verse like the one above. If you have children, ask them to contribute drawings showing these service providers doing their jobs well, or some other decorations, and then tape them to the basket! Share your experiences on social media with #LTBL.

5 – YOUR PRESENCE HAS IMPACT

6

SHARE YOUR LIFE WITH OTHERS

Share your food with the hungry,
and give shelter to the homeless.
Give clothes to those who need them,
and do not hide from relatives who need your help.

Isaiah 58:7

What an amazing calling we all have! We have been asked by our compassionate God to care for people in the raw struggles of their lives. In large scale, these issues are massive problems. But on a very personal scale, as we extend compassion to those in need, each hurt can be intimately and effectively addressed.

As God changes our hearts, we can't help but overflow in love towards others. With God in our lives, we stop pursuing indulgence because we know there are people who are hungry and need food. With God transforming our hands, we stop judging someone begging on the streets and we seek to provide them with shelter and equip them with skillsets to help them get back on the right path. With God urging our minds, we quit ignoring the kid who doesn't have clothes that fit, and we find creative ways to supply him with what he needs to succeed. With God pressing our souls, we stop holding grudges against our relatives, and we generously share from what God has graciously entrusted to us.

Shine the Light

1. Do you think our society sees Christians as generous or stingy?

2. In what ways has God blessed you beyond what you need? In what ways could you share with others?

3. The verse in this devotional is from a convicting section from the Bible. In this particular chapter, God is describing what kind of action (literally, what kind of "fasting") he wants from his followers. Which line from Isaiah 58:7 stands out to you as being the most important one for you to follow right now in your life?

4. What message would Christians be sharing with the world if they really took this verse seriously?

Lord God, in the beginning of time you spoke into the darkness and said, "Let there be light." Sadly, today, darkness has been creeping its way into the lives of people all over the earth. With my meager hands, and my compassionate heart, use me in service for others. Let me be a light in the darkness for someone you love today. Amen.

Share the Light

You can give all or part of your lunch to someone who needs it more than you do; you can ask your local children's shelter what size gym shoes they need donated or you can send a family member a care package in the mail. Do something for someone else today. Then, use #LTBL and share on social media about your experience.

6 – SHARE YOUR LIFE WITH OTHERS

7

Good News for a Change

*For once you were full of darkness,
but now you have light from the Lord.
So live as people of light! For this light within you
produces only what is good and right and true.*

Ephesians 5:8–9

Watch out! Today, alarmist arguments will try to hook you. Hysterical rumors will try to entice you. Provocative tabloids will try to snare you. Inflammatory remarks produce panic.

But take heart! There is more hope for our world than the news headlines may suggest. You can be confident that God will use you to share the light in this world because he is at work right now shining his light in you. Every time he pries a sin out of your life, every time he prunes away a fear, every time he molds your faith into shape, the Lord is preparing you. He asks you to join him in shedding light on lies because he knows he can empower you. God trusts himself to generate good work through you. God accepts the fact that he is pretty masterful at producing the right results in your life. He is at work removing the darkness in you so that his truth will be brilliantly evident through all you say and do.

This is the lesson of Katy Harkens, who prayed each night, diligently, for her ex-husband's soul.

7 – Good News for a Change

Shine the Light

1. Before he encountered God, the title of Sol Harkens' new book was *Aborting God: The Reasoned Choice*. This title was meant to be incendiary. What did this provocative title intend to accomplish?

2. Why do our media and news cycles pivot towards panic? Why did negative news become such a common standard of mainstream reporting?

3. Why does the phrase "Good News" carry an especially important message for our world today?

4. Isaiah 61:1, a passage that Jesus fulfilled, says this: "The Spirit of the Sovereign Lord is upon me, for the Lord has anointed me to bring *good news* [emphasis added] to the poor. He has sent me to comfort the brokenhearted and to proclaim that captives will be released and prisoners will be freed." Describe the "good" part of the "news" that Jesus has for our world.

Jesus, thank you for giving our world a shockingly different news cycle. When the rest of our world falls into the mire of despair and panic, you give us a lifeline of hope and restoration. I praise you today. And I want to share the light of your life with others. Amen.

Share the Light

Take a moment to consider how the Lord is shaping you into a person that doesn't fall prey to the panic-inducing headlines of the world. When all around you are words of doom and despair, what is a different message that can you share? Instead of promulgating negative information, find a heart-warming story in the news today, and share it with others in the grocery line, at the bank, or at school pick-up. When the worries of the world weigh others down, you can be a light in the darkness. Share some "good news" on social media, too, and use #LTBL.

7 – Good News for a Change

8

MY LIGHT AND MY SALVATION

*The LORD is my light and my salvation—
so why should I be afraid?
The LORD is my fortress, protecting me from danger,
so why should I tremble?*

Psalm 27:1

What causes you to be afraid? What stops you from doing what you are called by God to do? Is your obstacle confusion? Apathy? A lack of conviction? Is there some kind of distraction or are you upset at someone? Perhaps you struggle with a nagging sin? Are you worried about how people might respond to you?

In the movie, Sol is pursuing the wrong things—fame and fortune in defiance of God, but inside he is a broken man, very alone and fearful.

In the Bible, one of the most repeated phrases from God is this: "Don't be afraid." The Lord is flawlessly focused. God is passionate. He restores your verve for life. He fills your soul. The Lord heals your hurt and forgives your sin. He gives you strength to overcome your weaknesses. He offers companionship and invites you to join others in his mission. The Lord reassures you that he will respond to you with joy and blessing, even if others don't. So, what are you afraid of? In the Lord's power, live for Jesus today.

8 – MY LIGHT AND MY SALVATION

SHINE THE LIGHT

1. Psalm 27:1 describes the Lord's role in our lives in several different ways. In what ways is the Lord your light? Your salvation? Your fortress? Your protection?

2. Which one of those roles of God is the most difficult for you to personally accept? What stops you from noticing God in those roles in your life?

3. Isaiah 41:10 says this: "Don't be afraid, for I am with you. Don't be discouraged, for I am your God. I will strengthen you and help you. I will hold you up with my victorious right hand." Why do you think God had to say this sort of thing so frequently throughout Scripture?

4. Today, if given the opportunity to encourage someone, how could you help them overcome their anxiety or fear? In what ways does this devotional give you the strength to share God with them?

Dear Heavenly Father, you are my light and salvation. You are my strength and my shield. Through all that is ahead of me, help me stand confidently in you. Let me not falter nor bend to the fear of what is before me. Let me instead become a beacon of hope for others who face similar circumstances. Amen.

Share the Light

Think of a real-world concern that a friend is facing today. Knowing that the presence of Jesus is with you, think of at least one way that you could come alongside them today, then do it. Is it a phone call, an invitation to meet for a drink or lunch, or offering to run an errand for them or do a chore? Without betraying your friend's privacy, share your experience on social media and use #LTBL.

8 – My Light and My Salvation

9

WHAT THE LORD DOES, SO DO WE

So be careful how you live. Don't live like fools,
but like those who are wise. Make the most of every
opportunity in these evil days. Don't act thoughtlessly,
but understand what the Lord wants you to do.

Ephesians 5:15–17

Sol is stuck in a rut. He can think only of his loss, grief, and sorrow. Katy tells him that his misery and anger are consuming him. Speaking about their wonderful young son, she says, "Your bitterness has robbed you of the ability to remember that gift of joy."

Nothing in life is guaranteed. Therefore, be sure to value each blessing you have. Love your neighbor. Lift others up. Be an encouragement. Spend your time and your money wisely. Prioritize people over problems. Care for the sick. House the homeless. Advocate for those who can't defend themselves. Support the life of a child in the womb. Defend the cause of the orphan and the widow. Put others ahead of yourself. Fix your thoughts on what is true. Act with honor. Do what is right. Focus on what is lovely and pure. Hold up what is admirable. Think about things that are excellent. Praise only that which is worthy of praise.

These are the things the Lord himself does. So, we seek to live likewise. First, we love the Lord in everything we do and, secondly, we become a loving light for our neighbors in a darkened world. This is our calling. This is who we are.

9 – WHAT THE LORD DOES, SO DO WE

SHINE THE LIGHT

1. Philippians 4:8 says, "Fix your thoughts on what is true, and honorable, and right, and pure, and lovely, and admirable." Can you identify these things in your own life?

2. What are some things in your life that are the opposite of these? How could you stop thinking about these negative things?

3. Do you have any unresolved wrongs in your life? As someone who is a representative to God in this world, this has significant consequences. What steps could you take to begin resolving the wrong things?

4. How does allowing God's light to change you help you change others?

Heavenly Father, give me discernment to see what is good and determination to focus my thoughts on what is right in this world. Please, God, let your Spirit lead me to be a loving witness to my friends and neighbors today. Amen.

9 – What the Lord Does, so Do We

Share the Light

Contact a friend or family member right now and share the light of the hope that lives within you. Begin your conversation by saying something like this: "I was just reading my *Share the Light* devotional, and it prompted me to think of you. I want you to know that I think God made you very special. You are important to me. I'm thankful for your _____ [fill in the blank]." Use this opportunity to speak life and light into their situation today.

9 – WHAT THE LORD DOES, SO DO WE

10

God Produces Faith in Us

*You didn't choose me. I chose you.
I appointed you to go and produce lasting fruit,
so that the Father will give you whatever you ask for,
using my name.*

John 15:16

One thing that Katy does is pray, every day. She prays openly, so her sons can see and hear her. Her faith is on display, and it affects the boys, even as they struggle to find their own relationships with God the Father.

Faith is not yours; rather, faith is yours to give away. God did not give you your faith so that you could keep it private, never to show it, or shut people out of it. Faith is not something that people have as an individual property right. Yes, faith is personal, but it is relationally personal, not "isolation-ally" personal. It is shared. It's not stolen or hidden; it is lived out and offered up.

You have been entrusted with the good news of Jesus Christ. He has saved you, and he has loved you. He is challenging you, and he is calling you to make a difference in this world. He has given you faith in him so that you can give faith to others as well. Inspire people by the way you live out your faith today. Giving away your faith is one of the most important things you can do today.

10 – God Produces Faith in Us

Shine the Light

1. If God has called you to share his light with others, do you think he would equip you?

2. In John 15:16, Jesus compares the impact of our lives on others to "producing lasting fruit." Consider the process of producing fruit. How is our faith in Jesus like that?

3. In that verse, Jesus also says that our heavenly Father will give us whatever we ask for in his name. First, what does that tell you about who Jesus is? Second, what does that tell you about what he chose you to do?

4. If God is at the center of your life, he will produce things in you inwardly that will overflow outwardly. What sorts of things would you like God to produce in your life so that you can positively impact others?

Heavenly Father, in the name of Jesus I ask you today, produce your good work in me so that I may be a light to others in a dark world. May your life be evident in all I do and say, in all I think and dream, and in all the places I go. Amen.

SHARE THE LIGHT

The next time you are eating in public, visibly bow your head and give thanks for your food. If you are breaking bread with others, encourage everyone to join hands for saying grace. The seemingly small act of honoring God will encourage those around you. There is no need to be showy, but so often we are cowed into not honoring God because it isn't "cool." Pursuing Christ also takes leadership skills. Be bold, knowing that God has appointed you for such a time as this.

10 – God Produces Faith in Us

11

ANOTHER PLACE

> "Do not let your hearts be troubled. You believe in God;
> believe also in me. My Father's house has many rooms;
> if that were not so, would I have told you that I am going
> there to prepare a place for you? And if I go and prepare
> a place for you, I will come back and take you to
> be with me that you also may be where I am."
>
> *John 14:1–3, NIV*

One of the themes in *Let There Be Light* is the theme of death being just another existence, in the light with Christ. This fits with the whole reason Jesus came to the earth. He wasn't going to allow us to remain separated from him. His desire is to spend eternity with us, so he made a way possible. And just so we are aware of how serious he is, he lets his followers know that he is preparing a place for us. He assures us that he will come back to get us. He promises us that he will lead the way.

To be honest, his disciples had a difficult time wrapping their minds around this. They wanted to avoid that little problem of death. They refused to accept, at first, that Jesus himself had to die in order to bring his plan to fruition.

But later, after Jesus rose from the grave, they began to understand. By passing through death himself, Jesus created a way for us to have life.

11 – ANOTHER PLACE

SHINE THE LIGHT

1. During a near-death experience, Sol has a vision of his son Davey. The experience shakes him to the core. What do you think about life after death? What do you think it will feel like?

2. From what you know of Jesus, what kind of place do you think he is preparing for us? In what ways might that be different from what you might at first be inclined to want in a "place" in heaven?

3. What struggles or fears do you have about heaven? How can you relate to what the disciples may have been going through?

4. Look at the last comment Jesus makes in John 14:3. What do you learn about the point of heaven? What does this teach you about life itself?

Father, please help me find rest in you, to lay my burdens at your feet. When I fear, give me peace, and when I am worried, calm my mind. Amen.

SHARE THE LIGHT

Use the opportunity you have to spend some time with loved ones before they leave this earth. Donate some time at an elderly care facility or a children's hospital. Give dignity and show love to those who are dying. Cherish life and bring comfort the way that Jesus does.

11 – ANOTHER PLACE

12

THE MESSAGE OF CREATION

> The heavens proclaim the glory of God.
> The skies display his craftsmanship.
> Day after day they continue to speak;
> night after night they make him known.
> They speak without a sound or word;
> their voice is never heard.
> Yet their message has gone throughout the earth,
> and their words to all the world.
>
> *Psalm 19:1–4*

After he lost his son, Sol struggled to see God's hand in the universe. He refused to accept that a loving God, with the power to create everything, would allow his son to suffer and die.

However, when he had a vision of his son, the beauty of God's love and the brilliance of God's message overwhelmed him. The creative power of God's words, "Let there be light," which had launched heaven and earth into action, also rejuvenated his soul.

Has God ever shown you something that changed your life?

Look at the sky. What do you see? How far can you see? How does the sky look throughout the day? Watch the clouds form and pass by in the atmosphere. If it is rainy, marvel at the science involved. If it is stormy, be humbled by the power of the winds and weather fronts. If it is sunny, feel the warmth of the sun on your skin. Enjoy the light it gives to reveal God's creation. At night, consider the stars. How many are there? Examine the detail of the moon. Think of the importance of its pull on the earth, and the immense complexity of creation. What does it teach you about the message God has for you?

12 – THE MESSAGE OF CREATION

SHINE THE LIGHT

1. What is the most amazing thing to you about the universe?

2. What do you imagine exists in the universe beyond what you can see or understand?

3. Is it difficult for you to reconcile that God has the power to create everything, and yet there is suffering on the earth? Why do you think God lets bad things happen when his creation is so beautiful?

4. In Genesis 1 (NIV), God said, "Let there be light," and there was light. In fact, each time God said "Let there be … ," that thing came into existence. What do you wish God would speak into being, for your life?

Lord God, your power, your creativity and your love can be seen in the universe you have made. Today, let me encourage others to look up often and be amazed by you, just as I am now. Amen.

SHARE THE LIGHT

If you go into any workplace today, make a point of asking someone how they are doing, and really listen to the answer. Show others you care about them, by truly investing the few moments it takes to hear their struggle. Use your time to be uplifting to them, focusing outwardly instead of inwardly. Use #LTBL to post some of your ideas on social media.

12 – THE MESSAGE OF CREATION

13

SHARING GOD'S LOVE IN TIMES OF GRIEF

> Rejoice with those who rejoice;
> mourn with those who mourn.
>
> *Romans 12:15, NIV*

Both Sol and Katy are grieving the loss of their oldest boy, eight years later. Sol wallows in his grief, but Katy has determined to make a life for herself and her two younger boys. Grief is a very personal journey, and people handle it differently, in their own ways. But just because grief is personal doesn't mean we can't help those who are suffering.

A friend of mine lost her father. With two small kids, it was all she could do to make funeral arrangements, and care for her little ones. I stopped by the widow's house for a visit, and noticed all the dead and dying flowers. My heart bounded into action. I organized all the cards, cleaned up a bit, and threw away all the dead blooms. My friend was so grateful! Distraught over losing her dad, she didn't have the emotional energy to even start to deal with the many regular, practical tasks. Seeing her mother's house looking better gave her the impetus to start handling other matters for the household. It also gave me something concrete that I could do, instead of sitting and simply reciting platitudes and heartfelt, but unhelpful, comments.

13 – Sharing God's Love in Times of Grief

Shine the Light

1. When others approached you in your times of grief, what was helpful and what wasn't?

2. Sometimes the most powerful thing we can do for someone who is grieving is to simply be there for them. I remember a story of someone who went to a friend's house and polished their shoes for the funeral. Nobody would have thought to do that. He didn't offer; he just declared that was what he was there to do. And all the kids' shoes got polished that night. What are some thoughtful ways that God has gifted you to help someone through their grief?

3. How could our attempts to comfort someone who was grieving accidentally become a burden on them? What could you do to minimize the burden and emphasize your helpfulness?

4. If someone is mourning, what advice does Romans 12:15 give us? How could you do that?

※

Dear Jesus, give me an attentive spirit towards those who are hurting. Let my focus be not on myself, but on those you've placed in my path. Give me your words, your hands, and your heart for them today. Amen.

Share the Light

Death is difficult. It reminds us of our own mortality. But as Christians, we have faith in a life more abundant and everlasting. Do you have an aging person or someone mourning in your life? Speak to them about their fears or concerns—start the conversation, and allow them to share with you. What hope do you have in Christ that you can share with a grieving world?

13 – SHARING GOD'S LOVE IN TIMES OF GRIEF

14

TEMPERING YOUR TEMPER

Short-tempered people do foolish things,
and schemers are hated.

Proverbs 14:17

Jesus wants you to shine his light in the world. His light is patient and kind, clear-headed and pure-hearted. His light is not an attitude that mangles and messes the lives of others. Unfortunately, all too often, people let their tempers get the upper hand. Actions done on a short-fuse spread angry foolishness. Angry foolishness spreads angry hurt. Angry hurt spurs hatred.

People who are quick to anger inevitably do really stupid things, which in turn causes them to scheme and worm and twist things for their own protection and gain. Worse yet, those who react by scheming more conspiracy, more idiocy, or more lies in order to protect their own agendas spread further darkness all around them.

Those who follow Jesus are called to live in love. Jesus said to his disciples that their love for each other would prove to the world that they were his followers (John 13:35). Even in moments of fear and loss, an angry temper should not to be the first level response. Christians are called to be a light to the world, reflecting Jesus into the darkness. They are not supposed to be dispensers of darkness themselves.

14 – Tempering Your Temper

SHINE THE LIGHT

1. Gut check: What causes you to lose your temper? When do you struggle to keep your head cool? Who are the people that are most-likely to make you hot-headed?

2. Another uneasy question: When you lose your cool, what do other people see you do or hear you say?

3. When something or someone makes you angry, how do you wish you would respond? In what ways would you like to be more reasonable or mature in your anger?

4. What are some strategies that would help you de-escalate your anger? In other words, when you feel your *temper*ature getting out of control, what steps could you take to cool yourself down?

Lord Jesus, forgive me for those times when my temper is short. Give me a deeper patience and maturity so that I can respond to difficult moments with your wisdom. Please, guide me by your Holy Spirit, to use clear-headed words with a pure-hearted attitude. In your power, keep my head cooled by your love. Amen.

SHARE THE LIGHT

Think ahead to those things or people that will test your temper. Anticipate the battle that will rage in your own heart and head, and consider your adversary as a child of God, instead. Prepare yourself with some de-escalation strategies so that when those trigger moments occur, you will respond with the light of Jesus rather than a flash of anger.

14 – TEMPERING YOUR TEMPER

15

Spotlight

*All who do evil hate the light and refuse to go near it
for fear their sins will be exposed.
But those who do what is right come to the light so others
can see that they are doing what God wants.*

John 3:20–21

Have you ever been working in a darkened room, your eyes perfectly adjusted to the strain of the shapes and shadows, when suddenly, someone flips a switch to turn on the light?

I remember once working on a dark stage, but then a technician turned on the spotlight, cutting a brilliant path through the darkness. My natural first reaction was to flinch by shutting my eyelids tight and turning my head away. It's a wild reflex. If you were recording that moment you'd have seen my face wince and my eyes squeezed shut. I shielded myself from the glare of the bright beam. Remarkably, in that moment, even with my eyes clinched shut, I could still see the image of the spotlight dancing behind my eyelids.

Jesus is like that spotlight. And when he shines into the darkness of our actions, or the gloom of our lives, the glare can be painfully intense. But the light of Jesus is so very good, too. It was His light that illuminated the earth at creation. It was his light that led God's people to freedom from slavery. It was his light that represented the greatness and love of God throughout the entire Bible. His light helps us see things the way they really are.

So, adjust your eyes to the light of Jesus today. See his glory. Look at the beauty of his creation. Notice the worth he gave to every person. Don't recoil back into a shadow of who you were made to be.

15 – Spotlight

SHINE THE LIGHT

1. What good things could you do today so that others would see God's light and be encouraged?

2. What if everyone who knew what was right did that? Can you think of a way to shine His light more gently, without making people flinch?

3. Imagine God suddenly turning a spotlight onto our society. What things do you think would recoil in fear of being exposed?

4. Gut-check question here: If God were to shine a spotlight onto your soul, what things would make you flinch and turn your head away? Do you ever shy away from shining the light of God because you don't want people to react negatively or get mad at you?

Dear Jesus, don't let me get comfortable wandering around in the darkness. Shine your light so that I can see. Let my eyes adjust to your brilliance. And let me become a light to others through the good works you produce in me. Amen.

Share the Light

Grab a small flashlight and carry it around with you all day. If you find yourself shrinking back into darkness, turn it on as a reminder that God wants to light your path. Share this tool with others, as well. Also use it as a reminder to do good things that will be a light to others. The spotlight of your life might just be the surprising prompt they need to get out of darkness, themselves.

15 – SPOTLIGHT

16

CLEANING UP MESSES

> Oh, give me back my joy again;
> you have broken me—
> now let me rejoice.
> Don't keep looking at my sins.
> Remove the stain of my guilt.
> Create in me a clean heart, O God.
> Renew a loyal spirit within me.
>
> *Psalm 51:8–10*

There is a scene in *Let There Be Light* that shines light on the folly of our human efforts to clean up the mess of our lives. It comes at a moment when the veneer around Sol has begun to crack. He's made a mess of his marriage, of his family, of his career, of his relationships, and of his own soul. Late at night, he tries to wash away the detritus with alcohol and pills in front of the TV. On the screen, a late-night infomercial hawks a new magical cloth called a "Wipe Wowie." Sol, the brilliant atheist whose arguments against God convinced the masses, sits "zonked" in front of the TV. He gives in to the gimmicks of the carnival salesman and orders six cases of the "miracle" cleansing towels.

As Christians, we understand that no human effort can cleanse the mess of our lives, not even "Wipe Wowies." Oh, they might pick up some spills or fix some small mistakes. But Sol's personal healing couldn't begin until he realized his need for forgiveness. His soul couldn't be brightened by any man-made miracle-cure or magic potion. As the movie reveals to us, he needed the posture of a broken heart and the discovery of God's love.

16 – CLEANING UP MESSES

SHINE THE LIGHT

1. What messes exist in your life?

2. In his grief, Sol carried some very heavy grudges. What grudges might you carry that you should seek to resolve?

3. Do you know someone who is dealing with a mess in their life? How could you help show them the way toward forgiveness and healing?

4. Do you know someone who is grieving? Can you think of something you can do?

Heavenly Father, you alone can clean up the mess of our lives. Please forgive me for the times I've argued against you, for the moments I've hurt those close to me, and for the seasons where I've tried to fix it all without your help. Create in me a clean heart and renew a right spirit within me. Thank you for offering healing for my soul. Amen.

16 – Cleaning Up Messes

Share the Light

Down the road from our house, there was an entry to a park where people had carelessly discarded their trash. I took the kids there one day, armed with some garbage bags and kitchen gloves, and we cleaned up papers, cans, and bottles. A woman stopped to watch for a moment, then exclaimed, "You guys are fantastic! Thank you!" Find some place near you that might benefit from a quick clean up, and experience that fresh feeling of simply being effective and improving the lives of those around you.

16 – CLEANING UP MESSES

17

Your Calling from God

*Jesus says, "Look! I stand at the door and knock.
If you hear my voice and open the door, I will come in,
and we will share a meal together as friends."*

Revelation 3:20

You were created to live a life that shines the light of God. You were made to be radiant, to brighten up what is around you, and to be a reminder of the glory of the Almighty. As a Christian, you were meant to be provocative.

The word "provocative" simply means to "call forward." It recognizes your God-created purpose for activity and ministry. You were created to be called and you were called to be creative. You have been called forward to shine light on how life is to be lived on this planet. Jesus didn't make you to wander your days in darkness; rather, he made you to live them in the light of his life.

Katy understood this, and so, while she prayed for Sol, and challenged him in how he lived his life, she also waited for the right time to act, to provoke him to answer the door. And when a near-death experience created the door for him to gaze through, Katy sought the opportunity to introduce Sol to Pastor Vinny.

Jesus calls you forward. His voice extends an invitation to dinner, shared with friends, empowering you to give life to others. If you hear his voice, open the door to his presence in your life.

17 – YOUR CALLING FROM GOD

SHINE THE LIGHT

1. What do you think Jesus means when he says, "I stand at the door and knock?" (Rev. 3:20, NIV)

2. When someone "opens the door" to Jesus, what new reality are they invited to embrace? How is this different than the life they had before?

3. Have you ever thought about the word "provocative" like this before? How does it change your idea of being a Christian if you are "called forward" by Jesus?

4. Do you know anyone who has closed the door to Jesus? What do you think could help them open up?

Jesus, encourage me to respond to your life-giving call. Embolden me with your wisdom and love. Open up my life towards others so that they may see your light in me. Amen.

SHARE THE LIGHT

Pray for a friend who could use a positive nudge. Then call that person and ask them to share a meal with you. Witness to them by simply offering your support and confidence, but be sure to mention the source of all your hope: Jesus Christ.

17 – Your Calling from God

18

LIFE IS PRECIOUS

*For God so loved the world that he gave his one
and only Son, that whoever believes in him
shall not perish but have eternal life.*

John 3:16, NIV

We have eternal life because of what God has done. Because Jesus is our Savior, we know that we will live beyond what we see here and now on earth. In the greatest act of mercy and love ever demonstrated, Jesus allowed himself to die on the cross so that our lives would not have to be wasted.

In 2 Peter, we are told that God doesn't want anyone to perish. Life is a precious gift from God. We should not waste a moment of it.

Pastor Vinny said to Sol, "The Big G's love for mankind was so perfect, and His Son's love was so perfect, that He gave His only begotten Son, so that the rest of us might find Salvation." Pastor Vinny also shared that we can be "bathed in the light and love of our Lord and Savior."

When Sol was baptized, Pastor Vinny asked him, "Sol, do you accept the Lord Jesus Christ as your Lord and Savior?" Sol answered, "Yes."

Take a moment today to brush up on the simple Gospel. Read the third chapter of John and let it bring God's light into your heart. "Anyone who believes in God's Son has eternal life" (John 3:36).

18 – Life Is Precious

Shine the Light

1. What sorts of activities do you waste your time on?

2. What sorts of attitudes do you have that are a waste of time: worry or anger, perhaps? Consider for a moment why these attitudes of your heart end up hurting the preciousness of life.

3. Have you ever seen someone "waste away"? What was that like? What made that circumstance so difficult?

4. What is the opposite of waste? How could you show someone today that they are worth saving?

Heavenly Father, thank you for loving this world so much that you would send your Son to save us. You have shown us that this world is worth the fight. Empower me to treat others with the same preciousness that you have given to me. Amen.

SHARE THE LIGHT

We are a Christian nation of charity and volunteers. That's why when disaster strikes, the world turns toward the United States for assistance. Find a local charity that needs hands-on help, and offer an hour this week. Use your time to meet people, and minister to them by virtue of your presence. Use #LTBL, and share your experience on social media.

18 – Life Is Precious

19

MAKE IT REAL

> And then he told them,
> "Go into all the world and preach
> the Good News to everyone."
>
> *Mark 16:15*

Did you notice how Pastor Vinny talked about faith in *Let There Be Light*? At one point he says to Sol, "Jesus gets whacked…." This was Vinny's way to communicate that Jesus was unfairly executed on the cross. Sol, somewhat surprised, remarks, "I've never heard it put that way."

A lot of terms and issues in the Bible seem distant and detached, but they aren't. When we put things into everyday vernacular, we can see that Jesus' teaching still applies directly to who we are and what we are going through.

For instance, "Thou shalt not covet" sounds vague and restrictive, but in essence, it means don't waste time wishing you had what others had. Instead, simply focus and work toward having the things that you want.

Pastor Vinny says that he "didn't come to Jesus in any moment of epiphany." No, he just needed to know that Jesus was real. He needed to know that faith in Jesus worked for him in the way he spoke and the way he experienced the raw reality of life.

SHINE THE LIGHT

1. Maybe you don't feel prepared to shine the light of God into the world around you. Maybe you think you need to get better at praying first. Or maybe you think you don't know enough of the religious terms or practices, so someone else would be better at sharing faith in God than you. In what areas of your faith do you feel inadequate?

2. How does the message of this devotional help inspire simple ways you can speak about your faith?

3. If someone asks you what salvation means to you, in your own words, how would you explain it?

4. If you were given two minutes to share about who Jesus is and why he is relevant to your life, what would you say?

God, thank you for being real to me right now in this moment. Thank you for understanding me and where my I am in my life. Please help me embrace you unashamedly and whole-heartedly. Amen.

SHARE THE LIGHT

In your own words, write down the message of the Good News of Jesus. Consider what Jesus did for the world and how that impacts you, personally. Put it in an envelope and mail it to someone. Share it on social media for others to see, using #LTBL.

19 – Make It Real

20

Light Shining in Us

> We now have this light shining in our hearts,
> but we ourselves are like fragile clay jars containing
> this great treasure. This makes it clear that our
> great power is from God, not from ourselves.
>
> *2 Corinthians 4:7*

We wish we could be superheroes with insurmountable strength, but our power is fleeting. Our ability to control our health, our circumstances, and our relationships is limited. Our hearts are not made of steel. They are flesh. And they are fragile.

When Sol finally admits his frailty and inadequacy in light of God's powerful grace, he has an epiphany that changes him from selfish to selfless, from self-serving to a servant of others, including the family he had previously all but abandoned. This is the power of grace, and the fragility of the human heart.

It's humbling, but following Jesus requires us to admit that our power does not come from ourselves. This is good news! When others see the powerful light of God shining in our fragile hearts, they are transformed by his greatness shining in our weakness. The much-needed enlightening truth for our world is that real people with real concerns will find real restoration in God's light.

20 – Light Shining in Us

Shine the Light

1. In what areas of your life do you feel fragile?

2. What causes someone to pretend like they have their lives altogether or to think that everything is under control?

3. In what ways is God making his home in you? What remodeling or rearranging might he still want to do?

4. Who do you know who needs the "treasure" of God within them? How could having God's great power in them be just what they need right now?

Dear Jesus, what I have to offer is not perfect, but please make yourself at home in me. And as you do, please work in me so that I may be a source of restoration for others. Amen.

20 – Light Shining in Us

Share the Light

If you want a lasting visual of this amazing verse, find a clay pot and put something valuable in it. Place it somewhere in your home where it will remind you of how "we are like fragile clay jars containing this great treasure." Also, consider doing the same thing for someone special in your life. Somewhere on their jar write 2 Corinthians 4:7. Inside their jar, place a gift card or a plant or another personal, meaningful gift. Let them know that you have one just like it.

20 – Light Shining in Us

21

SHARE YOUR FAITH WITH OTHERS

> Then Jesus cried out, "Whoever believes in me
> does not believe in me only, but in the one who sent me.
> The one who looks at me is seeing the one who sent me.
> I have come into the world as a light, so that no one
> who believes in me should stay in darkness."
>
> *John 12:44–46, NIV*

When Sol breaks down, realizing that the vision he had of his late little boy was a gift, sent by God to an undeserving sinner, he sobs, "Oh, my God!" And Pastor Vinny comments, "He is your God, Sol, and he's holding out his hand to you."

Sin means missing the mark. God set a good goal for us. But when we took aim, we missed. The distance the arrow falls from its target is called the "sin distance." This is a picture of how we are separated from God. The Bible declares that everyone has sinned and "fallen short of the glory of God" (Romans 3:23). The target was life, but we chose to stray away (Isaiah 53:6). And yet, God demonstrates his own love for us in this: "While we were still sinners, Christ died for us" (Romans 5:8, NIV).

When God created the world, he tackled the void of darkness and said, "Let there be light." God never stopped doing that kind of work. He just asks that we look to him. Jesus came into the world as a light, so that those who have missed the mark should not stay in darkness, but by believing in him, have eternal life.

21 – SHARE YOUR FAITH WITH OTHERS

SHINE THE LIGHT

1. Have you ever lost hope because of your sin, and then found your hope renewed because of God? What made that experience possible?

2. Jesus said that whoever looks at him is seeing God (the one who sent him). Why do we need to look at Jesus to see God?

3. During an especially important conversation in the movie, Pastor Vinny said to Sol, "He is your God, Sol, and He's reaching out His hand to you." Why is it necessary for a sinful person to come to this realization?

4. Overcoming sin in our lives is onerous. Thankfully, we have a Savior who bore our sin on his shoulders. Take a moment to give thanks to God for the terrible beauty of the cross.

※

Lord Jesus, forgive me of my sin. Put me back on target day after day. Thank you for bearing my sin on the cross. I believe in you. Amen.

Share the Light

There are many organizations that provide our troops with care packages. Find one and offer your time or some donations, to help them send our servicemen and women some comforts from home. Take a moment and write a thank you note or two, sharing some love and appreciation for the freedom we enjoy in this country (and for their part in securing it).

21 – Share Your Faith with Others

22

Let There Be Light

*For God, who said, "Let there be light in the darkness,"
has made this light shine in our hearts so we could know
the glory of God that is seen in the face of Jesus Christ.*

2 Corinthians 4:6

Winter in the Northern Hemisphere can be dark. The daylight is shorter. The nights are longer. At the darkest time of the year, couldn't we use the reminder that Jesus came to bring the world light?

The very same One who created the light when there was nothing but darkness is shining his light into your heart today. If the vast darkness before time could be overcome by his brilliance, imagine how brightly Jesus could shine in you today. The warmth of his light melts icy exteriors. The brightness of his light causes dark shadows to flee. The clarity of his light clears up murky thoughts. While our world may be corrupted and confused, God's light reveals his truth and gives understanding. In fact, in our home, we've made a tradition of setting up our Christmas lights before Halloween!

It's no wonder Jesus is called the "Light of the World." The Bible teaches that darkness just doesn't understand the light—it misunderstands it, to be more precise. Darkness thinks it knows how Jesus works but is totally blindsided by his brilliance again and again. Darkness tries to hide but quickly discovers it can't. So, let there be light in your heart today. Allow the glory of God that is seen in the face of Jesus to shine his light in you.

22 – Let There Be Light

Shine the Light

1. Do you, or does anyone you know, suffer from SAD (Seasonal Affect Disorder)? This is when someone grows melancholy or depressed during the winter months. Why do the long, cold, dark days of winter drain enthusiasm of life out of so many people?

2. With the darkness of winter in mind, what makes the tradition of putting up Christmas lights such an enjoyable contrast?

3. How is the birth of Jesus, so small and fragile in the grand darkness of the world, such a world-changing event?

4. 2 Corinthians 4:6 says that God "has made this light shine in our hearts so that we could know the glory of God that is seen in the face of Jesus Christ." Describe what you think the face of Jesus looks like and why his face would reveal the glory of God to the world.

Dear Jesus, shine brightly in me and through me today. When others see me, let them see you in me. Amen.

Share the Light

In order to brighten up a friend's heart today, do one of these things: If it's sunny, invite a friend to sit in its warmth with you. If it's cloudy, invite a friend to sit by a bright, warm lamp or a nice fireplace. Share the words of 2 Corinthians 4:6 with them and let them know that God put them on your heart.

22 – Let There Be Light

23

Light for My Path

*Your word is a lamp to guide my feet
and a light for my path.*
Psalm 119:105

After a long day of travel, I arrived at my destination tired, but wired. I had been cooped up on a plane for too long, and needed some fresh air. In the waning light of day, I went for a jog on some trails, under the trees. The park was unfamiliar territory for me, and as I ran on the dirt path, I failed to see a root sticking out of the ground, in the longs shadows beneath the thick branches. I stumbled and fell, ripping gashes in my knee and elbow, and feeling stupid, to boot. Limping back home, I resolved to be more careful in the future, about where I ran.

Runners should choose well-lit paths for each step. And yet, so many people run through this life in the dark. They stumble when they could stride. They fall in dangers that they could have seen coming. They trip into snares that they could have avoided. They know they were created to run, but they have yet to know what it means to run free.

God's word is a lamp for our feet and a light for our path. It's like a map, revealing the way, the truth, the life. God's word enables us to do what we were created to do. Run with God.

SHINE THE LIGHT

1. If you can, take a moment today to skim through Psalm 119. What do you see there about how God's word (or "command" or "law") lights your path?

2. Do you have a pattern for reading God's word in the Bible? What could you do to make reading the Bible more of a habit?

3. What struggle do you have that causes you to stumble in your faith? In what ways could that struggle be considered a darkened path?

4. Think of your neighbors. Are there some ways that you are shining a light on their paths?

Jesus, let my eyes see where you are leading and let my feet find their traction in the path you have for my life. May your word guide the direction of my life today. Amen.

23 – Light for My Path

Share the Light

In church this week, take your day to volunteer to work with the children's ministry. Children often enjoy getting to know new people, so bless them with another voice this Sunday. Offer to serve, instead of being served, and see how it makes you feel, and how it affects those around you.

23 – Light for My Path

24

GOD IS OUR HERO

> He heals the brokenhearted
> and bandages their wounds.
> He counts the stars
> and calls them all by name.
> How great is our Lord! His power is absolute!
> His understanding is beyond comprehension!
>
> *Psalm 147:3–5*

Seven-hundred years before Jesus was born, there was a remarkable prophet named Isaiah. He described the Savior of the world as a child who is "given to us." He said that this child will be called "Mighty God" ("*El-Gibbor*") and have a fair and just kingdom that will never end.

El is the Hebrew word for God. Isaiah never uses it in reference to anyone other than the one true God of Israel. For Isaiah to use this title upon a child is absolutely astonishing. The reason people in the future will rejoice, the reason darkness will be destroyed, the reason light is coming into the world, is because somehow a child who is God himself will overturn all the consequences of sin and despair and distress and misery.

And this God is mighty. *Gibbor* literally means "hero." This child is the hero God. Are you walking in darkness? Don't fear, because God will give you light! Are you oppressed? Hang in there, for God is coming to the rescue. Is your soul imprisoned? God will free you! Are you struggling? God will revive you! He is the hero God who comes to save the world.

Shine the Light

1. Describe the miracle of Christmas. How could a child actually be called "Mighty God"—especially in the monotheistic Hebrew worldview?

2. Alongside "Mighty God," Isaiah also says that this child will be called "Wonderful Counselor," "Everlasting Father," and "Prince of Peace." What do these titles reveal to you about Jesus?

3. What aspect from this devotional do you need to embrace the most today?

4. God is going to be the hero of the story. Does this truth reflect the way you live your life?

Jesus, if I am not blown away by who you are yet, get my attention today. In my life, I pray that I will let you be who you truly are. Amen.

Share the Light

Bake or buy some special cookies to share at your church or workplace. Put a note on them: "Baked with love" or "Sharing to show caring." Leave them out for everyone to enjoy. Share some photos of this on social media (#LTBL).

24 – GOD IS OUR HERO

25

THE INTENSITY
OF THE LIGHT OF GOD

*And here is the basis for their judgment:
The Light of God has now come into the world,
but the hearts of people love their darkness
more than the Light, because they want
the darkness to conceal their evil.*

John 3:19, TPT

We live in sunny California now, but Kevin is from Minnesota, where winters are legendary. During a heavy snowstorm, the roads can become a potent mess of salt, sand, and slush. Deep walls of snow bank both sides of a street. Traffic is snared by dangerous black ice. Brownish slop sprays up onto windshields, when the melting starts, and wipers and washer fluid are only half-effective at ridding the glass of its inevitable muddle.

When the roads are like this, the sun isn't always necessarily considered friendly. For instance, if the sun suddenly breaks through the clouds it can smash down on a slush-stained windshield, causing a temporary blinding sensation to a driver. It's as if the brilliance of the sun goes to war against the hardened snowy-sludge. Some drivers panic, clutching their steering wheels trying to regain control. In that moment, it's almost as if some drivers want to yell, "Go away, sun! I want the shadows!" In reality, however, what they really need is for the sun to warm the temperature enough for the sloppy mess to go away.

25 – THE INTENSITY OF THE LIGHT OF GOD

SHINE THE LIGHT

1. Can you think of a time when the sun blinded you? What did it make you want to do?

2. Can you think of a time when you didn't want to get caught doing something you shouldn't be doing? What was that experience like for you?

3. Why do you think people in our world so often choose to continue in the grime of their lives rather than live in the light?

4. What steps does a person need to take if they want to live in the light of God?

Jesus, don't let me be comfortable with driving with grime in my life. As difficult as it is, help me give in to your brilliance. Amen.

25 – The Intensity of the Light of God

SHARE THE LIGHT

Sometimes, before we can be a light for others, we need to let the light of God shine more deeply into our own lives. Is there an area of your life that you hope will stay concealed? Talk to a pastor or good friend about it and resolve it. Our secrets can be burdensome, but the light can relieve us of them and lighten our load.

25 – The Intensity of the Light of God

26

THE POWER OF FORGIVENESS

*Put on your new nature, and be renewed as
you learn to know your Creator and become like him.*

Colossians 3:10

Sol's son, Gus, asks him if his transformation is for real. After how badly Sol had treated Katy, Gus was having a hard time accepting that someone could actually change as much as Sol seemed to be changing. But Sol answers him with a question, "Do you believe God hears our prayers?" Sol implied that through himself, alone, this shift in attitude might be doubtful, but God is mighty enough to transform even the hardest of hearts.

I had an old feud with an acquaintance who had wronged me months before. She had spat nasty words in my face, in a deliberate attempt to provoke me into a fight, to which I responded in irritation and hurt. I carried anger in my heart, whenever I thought of her, for over a year, until one day, in my prayer journal, I spontaneously wrote, "I pray for her. Let her burden be light, and let your love shine into her heart, as I pray for it in mine."

This began a new period in my life. I prayed for her every day, and each day it became easier. Eventually, I forgave her, and I prayed for God to forgive me for responding with anger.

And He did!

26 – THE POWER OF FORGIVENESS

SHINE THE LIGHT

1. Have you ever seen anyone transformed by God like Sol was? How would you explain it to someone like Gus?

2. If God can create the universe out of nothing, imagine what he could do with something that already exists. If you let God do some recreating work in your life, where might he begin? What changes do you think he would make?

3. In Colossians 3:10, why do you think the apostle Paul said that you should "put on" your new nature. Is it something that can be "taken off"? To what degree is this new nature a choice of yours?

4. One of the ways that Sol demonstrates to Gus that his transformation is for real is by apologizing to him. He describes how he had mistreated them and their mom and asks them for forgiveness. What role does forgiveness play in the process of being given a new nature by Jesus?

God, by your Word, create in me a clean heart, and renew a right spirit within me. Let me be refreshed in my soul today. Draw me close to you and help me to share this newness of life with those around me. Amen.

SHARE THE LIGHT

Who have you wrongly offended recently? Reach out to them and ask for forgiveness. If given the chance, let them know that the reason you reached out is that God is working in your heart to overcome the mistakes you've made. Do you need to ask God for forgiveness? Do you need to forgive someone? Think about where forgiveness is needed in your life (granted or received), and then see the power of Christ to renew!

27

God Is with You

> I could ask the darkness to hide me
> and the light around me to become night—
> but even in darkness I cannot hide from you.
> To you the night shines as bright as day.
> Darkness and light are the same to you.
>
> *Psalm 139:11–12*

Connor wonders aloud why God's message to his dad was "Let there be light." He asks, "Why? Was it dark?" Gus curtly answers him that God wants Sol to spread the message of light that Jesus brought to mankind, and Sol backs him up. But Connor is not satisfied, because Sol seems such an improbably choice. Do you feel like you are not the best choice too?

And yet, the Bible is chock full of stories of God using imperfect people for his perfect plan. Trust in God to make your inferior efforts work for his lofty purposes. After all, as Pastor Vinny says, "Who better to choose than the biggest atheist of all?"

Psalm 139:7 concludes: "I can never escape from your Spirit! I can never get away from your presence!" If you feel alone, maybe this comforts you. Or, if you are trying to hide something, perhaps this makes you uncomfortable. Even if hidden within the darkest recesses of your soul—still you would find God looking for you there. There is no place you can go to escape his presence. This is a profound and terrifying truth.

27 – GOD IS WITH YOU

SHINE THE LIGHT

1. Sol tries to hide in the "best that science has to offer." Did this help him get away from God? Why or why not?

2. Sol also tries to hide from God through pills and alcohol. Why do people so often turn to these sorts of "remedies" to get away from God?

3. Sol also tries to find comfort in late night TV. Why couldn't he just turn it off? What was he looking for? Can you relate to this?

4. In the end, Sol discovered he couldn't hide from God. Why did this become a comforting truth to him?

Lord Jesus, I'm tired of trying to hide from you. In fact, I confess that I can't, so it's not worth trying. You are too great for me. You are too powerful, too wonderful for me to comprehend. To what darkness could flee from the light of your life? There is no place where you won't shine your love in search of me. Thank you for loving me that much. Amen.

27 – God Is with You

27 – God Is with You

SHARE THE LIGHT

Jesus goes to great lengths to reach you. Think of someone you know who either feels all alone or is trying to hide. Reach out to them right now. Either write a letter, give them a call, or visit them where they are. Invite a stranger in church to brunch after, and learn something about their lives. If you can't think of anyone, write a letter to someone in prison, and share a story of forgiveness and love. Boldly make the effort. Let them know you were reading this devotional and it reminded you that God reached out to you, so you wanted to reach out to them.

28

UNEXPECTEDLY EXTRAORDINARY

*The people who walk in darkness
will see a great light.
For those who live in a land of deep darkness,
a light will shine.*

Isaiah 9:2

Jesus was born into the lineage of David. David, who was both the sweet singer of Israel and God's beloved. David, who was also one of greatest sinners in the Bible. He betrayed his best friends, murdered, committed adultery, lied, connived, and schemed to get and hold power. David was rightly called a "man of blood." He sank so low he called himself "a song for drunkards."

David's grandmother was Ruth the Moabite, who had her own gut-wrenching life story. Other ancestors of Jesus in this lineage include Rahab the prostitute and Jacob the deceiver. Jesus' own mother, Mary, was a simple teenaged girl.

The message in the family line of the Messiah is that there is nothing you can do—no sin so great and no circumstance of life that is too lost—that God cannot redeem for his purposes. He will never give up on you or stop loving you. It's the same story in *Let There Be Light,* because it is timeless, tried and true.

If David could be the seed of the Messiah, if Rahab could have hope, if Ruth could find a fresh start, if Jacob could receive a new name, if Mary could carry him in his womb, then you, too, can be a servant of God.

Shine the Light

1. Does it comfort you or disturb you to know that Jesus was born into such a complicated family?

2. As Isaiah's prophecy about the Messiah indicates, the people of Israel had been walking in darkness, but they would see a great light. From what you know of the history of God's people in the Old Testament, why were the Israelites an unlikely source for the Savior of the world?

3. Why do you think God likes to use unexpected people in extraordinary ways?

4. How could God do unexpected, but extraordinary, things in your own life?

Lord, I praise you for loving those who are weak, restoring those who are broken, and providing a way for those who are lost. If the Messiah can shine in the midst of a messy family, then he can certainly shine his light through me. In my weakness, may your light be made clear. Amen.

Share the Light

Take a friend and stand outside a Planned Parenthood office, to pray for the patients and those who don't come back out alive. (Be sure you are on public property.) Ask God to minister to the young women who are deceived by the lies our culture has forced upon them. Pray for the young fathers who are excluded from the conversations. You can be the difference for someone who is hurting.

29

COMMUNICATING THE LIGHT

We proclaim to you what we ourselves have actually seen and heard so that you may have fellowship with us. And our fellowship is with the Father and with his Son, Jesus Christ. We are writing these things so that you may fully share our joy.

1 John 1:3–4

Katy and Sol create the "Let There Be Light" app so that people can shine the light of God into a dark world, literally. As the timer on the app counts down to "0" at midnight on Christmas Eve, they want people to use the flashlight link on the app. Their goal is to have a "band of light" evident from space that circles around the globe to highlight the birth of the Savior.

The early Christians probably would have loved this technology. Just imagine all the networking they could have done. People like Paul, Peter, and John wanted to share with others what Jesus was doing in their lives. You can feel their sense of urgency in the New Testament letters. If they could do what you and I can now do, they would have utilized mobile phones and apps, as well as a whole host of other social media platforms to get their message out to their friends. For instance, I have a young friend who plays online gaming, and he witnesses to his co-players while he does!

Writing letters, the old-fashioned way, was the closest thing the early church had to our modern devices. They had to use ink and paper (well, papyrus), but they did their best, and were very prolific. When God put something passionate and important on their hearts, they couldn't wait to write to their friends about what Jesus was doing in their lives.

29 – Communicating the Light

SHINE THE LIGHT

1. Think of all the creative ways that modern technology could be used to spread the light of God around the world. How would the first followers of Jesus have utilized these advances in communication?

2. How do you use social media? Is the message of Jesus evident? Is your fellowship with God visible? In what ways could you be intentional about sharing God's light through your social media platforms?

3. No technology, however, is a substitute for real conversation. Why does our online communication need to be backed up by in-person relationships?

4. If you were to share a verse or a message of hope on social media today, what would it be?

Jesus, let me use the opportunities I have to share with my friends what you are doing in my life. Amen.

Share the Light

Using whatever method of communication that you want, share with some of your friends what Jesus is doing in your life. When you are out in public, for instance, openly carry this devotional, or another one, or the Bible, to show others that doing good and following Christ is a choice that takes commitment and tenacity. On social media, use #LTBL to tell stories of your experiences.

29 – COMMUNICATING THE LIGHT

30

REPRESENTING GOD

> So we are Christ's ambassadors; God is making his
> appeal through us. We speak for Christ when we plead,
> "Come back to God!"
>
> *2 Corinthians 5:20*

In the movie, Sol moves from the extreme posture of aborting God to the opposite position of representing God. This fits with the Bible's understanding of the dramatic calling of someone who is transformed by God.

Dr. Fournier disbelieves Sol's transformation (and who could blame him), but he sagaciously points out that as a Christian, he is called to forgive, despite his reservations. Most of the Christian community probably feels the same way, but as we see in the apostle Paul's own story, the spiritual rebirth that Christ makes possible can cause astonishing transformation!

The apostle Paul calls us "Christ's ambassadors." An ambassador is a person who is sent by someone else as an official representative. In other words, what the ambassador does and says reflects back on the person who sent him, personally and professionally. So, it is important that the ambassador does and says only what accurately reflects the sender's positions, without causing any incorrect appearances or misunderstandings.

Now imagine that Jesus has asked you to be his ambassador (because he has!). He wants you to represent him where you live. As you interact with others, Jesus has given you his authority to share his words and customs. It's as if you are a citizen of heaven and have been sent to your family, your friends, your workplace, and your community, specifically to let others know what God is like. It's a lot of responsibility, but it is a high calling.

30 – Representing God

Shine the Light

1. Unfortunately, throughout history, some people who have claimed to represent Jesus have done some terrible things. How has this sort of misrepresentation hurt the spreading of Jesus's message?

2. What do you think it means to represent Jesus purely and share his message clearly?

3. Think in terms of God's character and God's commands. In what ways are you already representing God? In what ways could you improve in your role as his ambassador?

4. Where has God asked you to represent him? What do you think he is asking of you?

Lord Jesus, I don't deserve the title, but I am so thankful to be your ambassador. I accept the calling you have given me, and I accept all the help you will give me. I need it! Please guide me by your Spirit to let me represent you effectively in my words and actions. Amen.

Share the Light

How do your actions at work reflect the presence of God in your heart? What message has God given you the authority to share? Is there someone at work who would benefit from your helping hand? Invite them to meet up outside of work. Showing you care might be the best way to witness to those around you.

30 – REPRESENTING GOD

31

COMMIT YOUR LIFE TO GOD

> Commit everything you do to the LORD.
> Trust him, and he will help you.
> He will make your innocence radiate like the dawn,
> and the justice of your cause will shine like the noonday sun.
>
> *Psalm 37:5–6*

Tracee used to worry about any number of things. Distracted by the culture surrounding her, she placed her faith in the *here and now*, and things often didn't turn out the way she hoped. Then she watched Sol turn his back on his previous self, and she realized that was the right thing for her to do as well. As scary as that was, Tracee's faith in Christ grew, and she began to rely on His truth, not on things of this world, and she retreated from the realm of the of *here and now*. Her confidence in things unseen birthed a newfound sense of peace, and trust in God's good promises.

The issues you face today may not make much sense; in fact, they may create a struggle for you. You may feel blind to the way God is working and wonder what in the world is going on. Because faith is lived out in the raw, reality of everyday circumstances, the Bible reinforces the instruction to trust in God. Your daily actions are to be entrusted to the eternal scope of the Lord, not to the temptation of short-sighted understandings.

In the midst of your trials, know this truth: God sees your daily toil. He is aware that division and deviousness in this world detracts from your ability to live fully. He is aware that the sin and destruction of others hinders your own pursuits. God is fully cognizant that things don't always work out the way you want them to work out. So, trust everything you do to him because he is going to use your work to share his light in the world in which you live.

31 – Commit Your Life to God

Shine the Light

1. How is untested faith like a soup you never taste before serving?

2. If there is not testing in life, then what is the purpose of faith?

3. What is the hardest thing about trusting God during difficult times?

4. Read Psalm 37:5–6 a few times through. Which phrases stand out the most to you? Notice the instructions in the first half of the verse and the promise in the second half. What relationship do they have to one another?

Jesus, forgive me for so often leaning on my own understanding rather than on yours. Lord, I commit every action of mine today to your plan. May your will be done in my life as it is in heaven. Amen.

31 – Commit Your Life to God

Share the Light

God calls us to trust our daily routines to him so that our "innocence can radiate like the dawn" upon others. Commit each action today to the Lord. To help you keep this mind today, tie a piece of yarn around your finger, or your keychain, or somewhere you will notice it all day. Then share your experiences on social media using #LTBL.

31 – COMMIT YOUR LIFE TO GOD

32

WALK IN HIS LIGHT

*And the city has no need of sun or moon,
for the glory of God illuminates the city, and the Lamb
is its light. The nations will walk in its light, and the
kings of the world will enter the city in all their glory.*
Revelation 21:23–24

The Bible begins with the light of God and the Bible ends with the light of God. In between Genesis and Revelation, darkness wages war. It steals people into the shadows. It draws people away from enlightenment. It spreads fear. It causes people to cower. It attempts to extinguish the light of God.

And yet, Jesus, the Light of the World never fails in the battle. John tells us, "In him was life, and that life was the light of all mankind. The light shines in the darkness, and the darkness has not overcome it" (John 1:4–5).

God created this world so that we could walk in his light. The testimony of history is that God never relinquished this goal. He has always chosen to shine his light onto the soul of humanity, beckoning us to walk with him. He illuminates our way, so that we can see him clearly. In the end, as the beginning, he himself will be our source of light.

SHINE THE LIGHT

1. What do you think heaven will be like?

2. The old Irish hymn, "Be Thou My Vision," says: "May I reach heaven's joys, O bright Heaven's Sun! Heart of my own heart, whatever befall, Still be my Vision, O Ruler of all." With these lyrics in mind, why is it important to keep our focus on the light of God throughout our lives?

3. Describe, in real terms that anybody could comprehend, the battle between darkness and light. Give some true-to-life examples of this battle.

4. How does knowing the beginning and ending of the story help you walk through the difficult circumstances of middle?

※

Jesus, Light of the World, let me see you clearly. Let me walk with you, today, my steps brightened by your presence. When I lose my way, call me back. When I trip and fall, lift me up. May my stride reach heaven's joys. May my eyes keep you in sight. Amen.

Share the Light

Call a nearby nursing home and volunteer your services. Maybe someone needs some flowers, or would appreciate you reading to them. Bring the newspaper or a good book to share for an hour of your day, and then put your story on social media (and share by using #LTBL).

32 – WALK IN HIS LIGHT

33

THINK OF OTHERS

*Do nothing out of selfish ambition or vain conceit.
Rather, in humility value others above yourselves,
not looking to your own interests but
each of you to the interests of the others.*
Philippians 2:3–4, NIV

"Not everything's about you, Sol."

Perhaps it's ironic that the main character of the movie needed to learn that he wasn't supposed to be the central focus of his own life. It wasn't until he placed his wife and his sons ahead of himself that transformation truly started to take root in his life.

Being self-indulgent never wins. It makes people irritable and demanding. Have you ever heard of a celebrity who acted like a "diva?" Selfishness is like that. It eclipses any awareness of the needs of others. It makes a person lose sight of what it means to share this earth with others. Selfishness leads to unending quests of self-gratification, self-service, and a self-interest that discredits the rights or concerns of others.

A life lived for others, however, is freeing. When you lift others up around you, your heart is lifted with them. When you meet someone in their time of need, you are blessed. When you see serving a friend as an honor, your own self-esteem grows deeply. This is how Jesus lived. It is how we were meant to live as well.

33 – THINK OF OTHERS

SHINE THE LIGHT

1. Philippians 2:5 says, "In your relationships with one another, have the same mindset as Christ Jesus" (NIV). In what ways did Jesus embody an altruistic attitude?

2. How is a community changed when individuals live on behalf of one another, rather than obsessed with their own concerns?

3. How do you know when you are being humble?

4. How does humility shine the power of God?

☼

Lord Jesus, thank you for giving us the example of how to live for the sake of others. You gave your life on our behalf. You care for those in need. You hear our cries. You are patient. You are kind. You do not boast or envy. You forgive our wrongs and you are ever present for us. Let me share even a fraction of your level of love for others today. Amen.

33 – Think of Others

Share the Light

Brainstorm a list of at least ten things you could do to help others today. It could be as simple as taking a cart back from someone at the supermarket, holding a door open for someone, or paying for the coffee of the person after you in line. At the end of the day, check each one you were able to accomplish and share your story on social media, using #LTBL.

33 – THINK OF OTHERS

34

OVERCOMING DEATH

*Jesus said to her, "I am the resurrection and the life.
The one who believes in me will live,
even though they die; and whoever lives by believing
in me will never die. Do you believe this?"
"Yes, Lord," she replied, "I believe that you are the Messiah,
the Son of God, who is to come into the world."*

John 11:25–27, NIV

Let There Be Light does not shy away from the difficult reality of death. Christianity doesn't either. One of the reasons Jesus has such an important message for our world is that he deals directly with death. He knows the fear and anger it instills in us. He knows the disruptive impact it has on our families and relationships. And like us, he knows the grief of losing someone close to his heart. He has walked where we walk. He has mourned where we will mourn.

John 11:35 reports that "Jesus wept" (NIV). It's the shortest verse in the Bible, and yet it is one of the most profound. When his dear friend Lazarus died, Jesus grieved. He felt loss. His heart ached. He mourned with his friends and family. He faced death just as humanity did.

And yet, as Christians, we are able to say with the apostle Paul, "Where, O death, is your victory? Where, O death, is your sting?" (1 Corinthians 15:55, NIV)

SHINE THE LIGHT

1. How would you describe life after death to someone? What role does Jesus play in the passing from this life to the everlasting life?

2. The memory of those we've loved and lost impacts us. The people who have affected us in our lives change us as we go about our days, even after they are gone from this world. Think of someone you have lost. How could you honor them today?

3. Describe the bittersweet reality of having loved someone enough that you grieve the loss of their life.

4. What did Jesus mean when he said, "I am the resurrection and the life"? What comfort or hope does this bring you?

Heavenly Father, Psalm 23 says that even though I walk through the valley of the shadow of death, I will fear no evil. You walk with me. Your presence comforts me. You understand the beat of my heart and the thoughts of my mind. You prepare a place for me and anoint me as one of your own. Thank you for giving this world the hope it needs. Amen.

34 – Overcoming Death

Share the Light

Who is *missing* from your life right now, and what might you do to remind the world they were here? If you know someone who has lost someone or is currently grieving, let them know you are thinking of them today. Phone them, text them, or send them a card. Offer to run an errand for them. One way to share the light is by showing love and allowing others to feel the love that is Christ, through your investment.

34 – OVERCOMING DEATH

35

GOD'S PLANS INCLUDE YOU

*"Everyone who calls on
the name of the L ORD will be saved."*
Romans 10:13

Even when things around you, or in you, are messed up, there is a remarkable truth that still reigns: Jesus created this world so that he could hang out with you. There is also a second truth that is just as remarkable: God doesn't give up on his plans. And no matter what you are experiencing today, no matter what you are facing in this moment, it just so happens that you are in the blueprint of God's plans for this planet. That is good news indeed. And good news is what Jesus is all about.

Davey's young brothers knew this simple truth. Although initially they feared what was happening to their mother, in time they came to trust again in God. Children often have easier faith than adults. Try to make your faith like a child's.

Turn to the Lord today. Call on his name. Ask him to shine his light all around you and in you. This is what he wants for your life—it's why he created you in the first place. It is why he came for you, and it is why he called out on your behalf on the cross. It is why he conquered sin and death. Jesus made you, he loves you, and he plans to be a light in you for a dark world. Call on Jesus today.

35 – GOD'S PLANS INCLUDE YOU

SHINE THE LIGHT

1. Have you ever found yourself in trouble to a point that you needed to call out to someone for help? What was that experience like? What emotions did you have? What concerns did you face?

2. One of Sol's catchphrases in the movie is "aborting God." What if Sol had been right? What if God didn't exist? Or what if we could have stopped Jesus from dying on the cross to conquer our sin, to overcome our trouble? Who would you call out to then? Who could save us from our circumstance?

3. What trouble do you have today? How could you call out to the Lord and what would you ask of him?

4. If people don't hear about God's saving work, how could they believe in him? And if they don't believe in him, how could they call out to him in their time of need? These are the questions asked in Romans 10. That is why Jesus asks us to spread his name across the globe. What could you do today, to make this message known?

☼

Jesus, I call on your name today. Be with me in a renewed way. Make me right in your eyes. Make me mighty for your plans. And make me a light for this world that you love so much. Amen.

Share the Light

Sometimes, to share the light with others, we need to first remember to receive the light of God ourselves. So, for this devotional time, take a moment to call on the Lord. Reach out to him in a deep way. Let him know of your needs. Ask him to provide. Seek him with all of your heart. Then place before him the names of those in your life who need the light of his salvation.

35 – GOD'S PLANS INCLUDE YOU

36

SHARE THE GOOD NEWS

> How beautiful on the mountains
> are the feet of the messenger who brings good news,
> the good news of peace and salvation,
> the news that the God of Israel reigns!
>
> *Isaiah 52:7*

Katy comes to grips with her illness, and she desires to share the hope that exists in her heart. Her hope was a message of light for the world stumbling in darkness. Her hope isn't a wishful desire. Her hope is strength. Her hope is tested. Her hope was her firm foundation through times of disparaging heartache and broken relationships.

Katy's hope evidenced itself through her steadfastness. The fruit of her faithful walk with God, even through difficult times, had an undeniable impact on those who knew her.

At one point, Sol confesses that she "was always there for him." This reality overwhelms him. In the chaos of his journey, Katy was the reliable, consistent person that he really needed. Her faithfulness brought good news to his life. Her constant message of hope brought him peace and salvation. She became beautiful to him in a way that transformed him.

36 – Share the Good News

Shine the Light

1. What are some inappropriate ways that people share "news"? Do you fall into any of those patterns? How are Christians supposed to share the light?

2. What is the "good news" that God has for the world? Let's make this hit closer to home: What is the "good news" that God has for a friend or family member of yours who is struggling in darkness?

3. Have you allowed the good news of Jesus to transform you? What areas of your life could use a reminder of his good news today?

4. Katy shared the good news through the steadfast determination of a consistent life. How has God equipped you to bring his good news?

Lord Jesus, help me be so changed by your good news that I can't help but share it with others. Amen.

SHARE THE LIGHT

Are there opportunities in your non-religious social groups to share the love and light of Christ? If not, think of someone you will meet today, and invite them to a church service. Simply tell them the time and location, and say, "Everyone is welcome there." In order to share the good news about what Jesus has done, where do your "feet" need to go today? Through social media, use #LTBL; share any positive responses you get.

37

Whoever Has Jesus

> And this is what God has testified:
> He has given us eternal life, and this life is in his Son.
> Whoever has the Son has life; whoever does not
> have God's Son does not have life.
>
> *1 John 5:11–12*

Here's a beautiful reminder. God is going to spread the light. Yes, he asks us to do our part, but ultimately, he is the one who testifies concerning himself. He will make his message known. He will not let the darkness win. Never again will darkness cover the face of the earth. He will fight the battles. He will champion the cause of the weak. He will speak on behalf of the mute. He will restore sight to the blind. He will uplift those who have been knocked down. He will pierce the darkness with his brilliance. He will still the storms. He will testify: I AM who I AM.

So, when God says there is life through Jesus, believe him. When God says, whoever has Jesus has life, believe him. When God says he sees you, he loves you, he knows you, and he saves you, believe him.

SHINE THE LIGHT

1. What is God's testimony? What "faith story" does he have to share with the world?

2. If God is going to shine his light on this earth anyway, why does he still want you to be a part of it?

3. If you had two minutes to share with a stranger about your faith, what would your "testimony" be?

4. Imagine this scene for a moment: God has been called to the witness stand. You are the defendant. You are on trial. At stake is death or life. Darkness or light. What testimony would you want God to give? How does his testimony in 1 John 5:11–12 relieve your soul?

Lord God, thank you for your story of faithfulness. You are a witness to your own work throughout history. You have seen the truth of your Son and the life he has given through his death on the cross. I am freed from death because of your great testimony. Amen.

37 – Whoever Has Jesus

Share the Light

How did you come to hear about what Jesus has done? Who shared this message of hope with you? Who took the time to shine this light into your life? If you can, do at least one of these two things today: 1) contact the person who shared Jesus with you and let them know how thankful you are; 2) in the same way, reach out to someone with the life-changing good news about Jesus.

37 – Whoever Has Jesus

38

Hypocrite-Proof Yourself

*This is the message we heard from Jesus and now declare
to you: God is light, and there is no darkness in him at all.
So we are lying if we say we have fellowship with God but go
on living in spiritual darkness; we are not practicing the truth.
But if we are living in the light, as God is in the light,
then we have fellowship with each other, and the blood
of Jesus, his Son, cleanses us from all sin.*

1 John 1:5–7

Be real today. If you say you are a follower of Jesus, then do as he would do. Don't be all show. Have depth of character. Have integrity. Act on your words. Being authentic is all about honesty.

Faith requires actually putting yourself in action. Faith is risky because it takes proactive effort. Once Sol gave his life to Christ, he took steps to fulfill that promise, and Katy helped him. Together, they devised the app that they develop in the movie. At the end of the film, you witness the change in attitude that Sol reveals when he loses his true love, a complete departure from his response to the loss of Davey.

Like Sol, you also, must act in faith, putting one foot ahead of the next, trusting that each step is leading you where you should go next. Faith is not lazy. Faith does not sit around bored, just hoping something good might happen. It is not worried. Faith does not panic at what might occur. Faith is doing what you believe is true. If your faith is in Jesus today, then you will naturally act upon what Jesus is leading you to do.

SHINE THE LIGHT

1. James 2:14 says: "What good is it, dear brothers and sisters, if you say you have faith but don't show it by your actions? Can that kind of faith save anyone?" How would you answer that question?

2. Why are some people quick to criticize hypocritical Christians? Do they have a point?

3. There is an old song that sings, "They'll know we are Christians by our love." How does that work? What is it about "our love" that shows people we are Christians?

4. How is our "fellowship" with other Christians a key ingredient to sharing the light of God with our world?

Dear Jesus, let my words and actions match yours. Thank you for cleansing me through your blood, shed for the forgiveness of my sin. Let there be light in my life today as a result of what you have done. Amen.

Share the Light

Often, we are too afraid to speak up, even when we know the right thing to do. Be bold in truth! Pick one of these actions to follow through with today (and if you are asked, be ready to share the reason why you are doing it): Tell the (thoughtful) truth, jump in to help someone, confidently *choose* purity, leap to someone's defense, or reassuringly listen to a friend.

38 – HYPOCRITE-PROOF YOURSELF

39

LET YOUR LIGHT SHINE BEFORE OTHERS

You are the light of the world—like a city on a hilltop that cannot be hidden. No one lights a lamp and then puts it under a basket. Instead, a lamp is placed on a stand, where it gives light to everyone in the house. In the same way, let your light shine before others, that they may see your good deeds and glorify your Father in heaven.
—*Matthew 5:14–16, NIV*

The old children's song describes this with a light-hearted melody: "This little light of mine, I'm gonna let it shine … Hide it under a bushel? No! I'm gonna let it shine … Let it shine, let it shine." A bushel is a basket that held a measurement equal to about eight gallons of dry goods. The idea of the song is simply that no one would hide a candle under a bushel basket. Doing so would block the light and could be a dangerous fire hazard. No, that would be ridiculous. A candle that's hidden might as well not be lit.

For this reason, the final image of *Let There Be Light* is perhaps the most important message of the movie. It is a simple but world-changing call to action. It is a reminder that we shouldn't hide our faith in a dark world. The image contains these famous words from the book of Matthew: "In the same way, let your light shine before others, that they may see your good deeds and glorify your Father in heaven."

Jesus, the Light of the World, wants to brighten the world through you. Don't hide yourself, or your faith, away. Instead, let your light shine before others.

39 – LET YOUR LIGHT SHINE BEFORE OTHERS

SHINE THE LIGHT

1. Consider trying this: Light a candle then put a non-flammable bowl over it. Take a moment to notice how ridiculous that is.

2. Next, relight the candle, leave it uncovered, and let it shine as a reminder of what you were created to do.

3. What are some ways that you are tempted to hide your faith from others?

4. Brainstorm a list of at least seven small ways that you could "let your light shine" for someone to see.

Lord God, you have brightened my soul with the light of your life. Please, let me be a brilliant light to others today. This world needs more of your light. Give me the courage to shine for you. For your glory, Amen.

39 – Let Your Light Shine before Others

Share the Light

The next time you get an unhelpful sales clerk or rude waitress, take a moment to consider they might be struggling with heartache you don't understand. Try sympathy instead of indignation, and offer them an encouraging word. You'll feel better about yourself. Today, choose one action step from the list you developed of small ways you could "let your light shine," and put it into action. Afterwards, share about what happens through social media using #LTBL.

39 – LET YOUR LIGHT SHINE BEFORE OTHERS

40

Spreading the Band of Light

> This same Good News that came to you is going out all over the world. It is bearing fruit everywhere by changing lives, just as it changed your lives from the day you first heard and understood the truth about God's wonderful grace.
>
> *—Colossians 1:6*

You can't always see the impact you are having on those around you. The little things you do that don't make you famous, and that seem to go unnoticed, may actually be a catalyst for something greater than you could ever imagine. Sharing the light of God in this world sometimes means simply doing your part in living every day in the creative light of Jesus. By doing this, others can be changed by the authentic life that is evident in your integrity, in your joy, in your peace, in your words, and in your acts of kindness.

Sol's wife, Katy, had this kind of light within her. In dark times, she trusted the light. Her consistency enabled her husband to eventually see his way forward. Her every day faith, and the spark of her faithful vision, helped spread a band of light across the world.

Here's an encouraging reality: While each one of us lives out our faith in Jesus, there are millions of others who are also living out theirs. Millions of little actions become a gigantic world-changing movement. You are a part of something huge—the good news of Jesus transforming this world, one by one, little by little, person by person.

40 – Spreading the Band of Light

Shine the Light

1. If you could change anything about our culture what would it be?

2. How does God want to go about changing lives in our culture today? What part do you have in his plan?

3. For two-thousand years, the message of Jesus has spread bands of light across the world, one person at a time. Who shared this world-changing movement with you? How did they share the light of God with you?

4. What little things are you doing each day that could, in the long run, light a path forward for someone else?

Lord, thank you for changing my life from the inside out. You have been working on me, loving me, and motivating me to grow in the patterns of my faith. Please let me be consistent in the little things of each day so that over time it will have a huge impact on those around me. Amen.

Share the Light

How has this devotional, putting action to your faith, strengthened you or given you hope? Through either a message, a phone call, or in person, check in with someone you care about. Ask them how they are doing, and let them know that God put them on your heart. Share with them how putting action into faith has inspired you, and encourage them to do the same. Maybe offer them a copy of this devotional.

40 – Spreading the Band of Light

Afterword

Rescue Boats

There's a story that has travelled through the years about a man named Joseph stranded on his rooftop during a flood. In the morning after the big storm, a middle-aged man floats by clinging to a log. He shouts out to Joseph, "Jump in and hold on to my log, and together we will float to safety!"

Joseph replies, "No, thank you. My God will save me!"

A little later, a fisherman comes by in his rowboat and offers Joseph a ride to safety. But the forlorn man replies, "No, thank you. God will save me!"

As night falls, a helicopter pilot sees Joseph on his roof, the waters still rising, and drops down a rope for Joseph to grab onto. But Joseph waves him away, repeating, "I put my trust in God!"

Joseph later perishes in the churning waters, and being a confessing Christian, he immediately ascends into heaven.

"Why didn't you rescue me?" Joseph demands of God, disappointed and dejected.

God, long-suffering, answers, "I sent you a log, then a rowboat, and finally a helicopter! What more did you expect?"

Our point is simply that God uses us humans to be his hands and feet to both profess the gospel and enact it here on earth. We've all witnessed the incredible power of prayer put into action, such as the light literally coming back into the eyes of those suffering and the joy returning to those overcome by loss. Like the remarkable British boats of Dunkirk or the astounding American boatlift from Manhattan on September 11, 2001, we pitch in during times

AFTERWORD – RESCUE BOATS

of crisis. Heroism, however, cannot be confined to catastrophes, and Jesus saves even in periods of peace. You don't have to wait for misfortune or travel the globe to change the world. You can take steps in your own home, family, and community every day to make a difference and further the kingdom of God.

Franklin Graham's Samaritan's Purse (samaritanspurse.org) has Operation Christmas Child, a ministry delivering gift-shoeboxes to needy children around the globe.

Next time you buy a pair of shoes, save the box! Pack it full of Christmas surprises for a young person and drop it off at a local collection point. Samaritan's Purse has suggestions for what to pack on their website, so it couldn't be easier, and it's a lot of fun! It is also a wonderful way to get into the true Christmas spirit and to share that with your own children.

There are plenty of ways to reach outside yourself and serve others that are not too demanding or costly, and they can be incredibly fun and done year-round. *Share the Light* encourages you to put your feet to your faith, personally and immediately. Where might you pilot your "boat" to offer a rescue or just a ride to another shore? Do not wait to get started on your own journey to be a benefit to others, because in service we are ultimately made whole as human beings that are created in the *imago dei*. God wants to use you as his hands and feet.

Prayer is a powerful tool, but it must be combined with actions. Let us all *share the light* of Jesus Christ through our efforts on behalf of those among us who are hurting. Let us reach beyond ourselves, whether it be just down the street or across the globe, to help the light penetrate the darkness of this world.

Let us all become fishers of men, with our *hearts* and with our *boats*.

This book is dedicated to
Braeden, Shane, and Octavia,
and to the other parent–
I couldn't have done it without you, sweetheart.

ACKNOWLEDGMENTS

We would like to thank our Lord for modeling sacrificing self to benefit others, Ken Castor for his outstanding effort and contributions, and Suzanne, David, and Bill for their hard work and inspiration. Thank you.

ABOUT THE AUTHORS

Sam Sorbo studied biomedical engineering at Duke University before pursuing a career in entertainment. An award-winning actress, author, radio host, international model, and home-schooling mom to three children with Kevin Sorbo, Sam Sorbo authored *They're YOUR Kids: An Inspirational Journey from Self-Doubter to Home School Advocate* to empower parents to home educate. She followed up this book with *Teach from Love: A School Year Devotional for Families* (BroadStreet Publishing). She frequently speaks on education across the nation.

Sam co-wrote, produced, and co-starred in the 2017 feature film *Let There Be Light* (executive producer, Sean Hannity; director, Kevin Sorbo.) Her boys also acted in the film, making it truly a family affair. The award-winning film was the fourth highest grossing faith-based feature of 2017. For more information on Sam, go to www.SamSorbo.com.

Kevin Sorbo—best known for his titular role in *Hercules, the Legendary Journeys,* and as Captain Dylan Hunt in Gene Roddenberry's *Andromeda*—has been a driving force in Hollywood for over two decades. With a long list of acting, modeling, producing, and directing credits to his name, Kevin has built a career that resounds throughout more than 176 countries. Since focusing more on film-making, he has had the honor of working with some of Hollywood's most acclaimed, and he was honored by the MovieGuide™ Awards for "Most Inspirational Performance of the Year." Among myriad productions, he starred in the acclaimed *God's Not Dead*, which was dollar for dollar the most successful film of 2014.

In 1997, Kevin suffered three strokes resulting from an aneurism in his left shoulder. He tells the compelling story of his grueling recovery in his book *True Strength: My Journey from Hercules to Mere Mortal and How Nearly Dying Saved My Life*. He directed and starred in the feature film *Let There Be Light*, which he co-produced with his wife, Sam, and Dan Gordon.

Kevin proudly supports A World Fit for Kids, a successful mentoring program for inner-city teens and children. For more information about Kevin's illustrious career or his foundation, log on to KevinSorbo.net and WorldFitForKids.org.

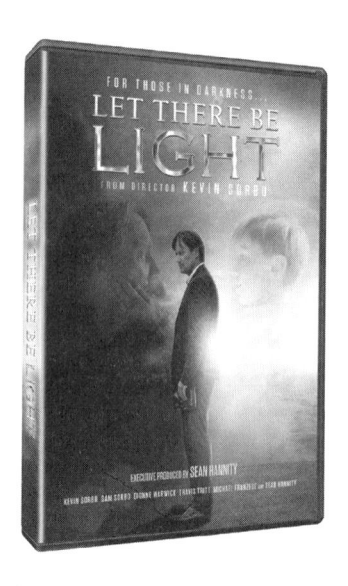

AVAILABLE ON DVD AND BLURAY

World-famous atheist Dr. Sol Harkins (Kevin Sorbo) delights in debating and defeating Christians but is emotionally empty. Isolated from Katy (Sam Sorbo), the wife he divorced following the harrowing loss of their first son, Sol is a lousy part-time dad to their two younger boys. His self-destruction culminates in a car crash that leaves him clinically dead for four minutes. The four-word message from that experience challenges his convictions, sending him into a panicked tailspin. Reluctantly leaning on his family's forgiveness, love, and faith, Sol struggles to find meaning and purpose in the words "LET THERE BE LIGHT."